Count Your Way through
Zimbabwe

by **Jim Haskins** and **Kathleen Benson**

illustrations by **Janie Jaehyun Park**

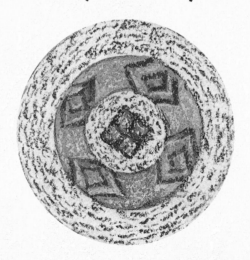

M Millbrook Press / Minneapolis

To Emilio and Josué -K. B.

To Anna -J. J. P.

Millbrook Press, Inc.
A division of Lerner Publishing Group
241 First Avenue North
Minneapolis, MN 55401 U.S.A.

Website address: www.lernerbooks.com

Library of Congress Cataloging-in-Publication Data

Haskins, James, 1941–
    Count your way through Zimbabwe / by Jim Haskins and
  Kathleen Benson ; illustrated by Janie Jaehyun Park.
      p.   cm. — (Count your way)
    ISBN-13: 978–1–57505–885–6 (lib. bdg : alk. paper)
    ISBN-10: 1–57505–885–5 (lib. bdg. : alk. paper)
    1. Zimbabwe—Juvenile literature. 2. Shona language—
  Numerals—Juvenile literature. Counting—Juvenile literature.
  I. Benson, Kathleen. II. Park, Janie Jaehyun, ill. III. Title.
  DT2889.H37 2007
  968.91—dc22   2005033163

Manufactured in the United States of America
1 2 3 4 5 6 — DP — 12 11 10 09 08 07

Introduction

Zimbabwe is a country in southern Africa. More than 12 million people call Zimbabwe home. Zimbabwe has an area of 150,803 square miles. It is a little bit bigger than the state of Montana. English is the official language of Zimbabwe. That is because Great Britain once ruled the country. The British brought the English language with them when they came to Africa. Most people in Zimbabwe speak English. But Zimbabweans usually use African languages in their daily lives. The most common African language in Zimbabwe is called Shona.

1 poshi (POE-she)

There is only **one** Victoria Falls. This huge
waterfall is located on the Zambezi River
in western Zimbabwe. Water from the
falls sprays high into the air. The mist
looks like smoke rising to the sky.
Zimbabweans call Victoria Falls
the smoke that thunders.

2 piri (PEE-ree)

Two favorite foods in Zimbabwe are *sadza* and *nyama*. Sadza is a very thick porridge. Zimbabweans roll sadza into balls and dip it into soups and stews. Nyama is the Shona word for "meat." Beef and chicken are the most popular meats in Zimbabwe—but meat is not a part of every meal. Cooks serve meat stews with sadza for a special treat.

3 tatu (TAH-too)

Three homes sit side by side in a farming village. Houses in Zimbabwe's villages are often round. They are made of mud, sticks, and straw. Families often live near one another. A brother and sister might live next door to their uncle, aunt, and cousins. Many people live in Zimbabwe's big cities. Most houses in the cities are modern. They look a lot like houses in the United States.

4 ina (EE-na)

Four countries border Zimbabwe.
They are Mozambique, South Africa,
Botswana, and Zambia. Zimbabwe
is landlocked. This means that there
are no oceans or seas surrounding
the country.

ZAMBIA

MOZAMBIQUE

Zambezi River

Victoria
Falls

ZIMBABWE

BOTSWANA

SOUTH AFRICA

5 shanu (SHA-noo)

Five popular arts in Zimbabwe are pottery, textiles, basket making, beadwork, and sculpture. Artists make pots for cooking food. They sew beautiful clothing and blankets. They weave baskets for storing items or catching fish. Some artists sell beaded jewelry to tourists. Sculpture is a newer art. People all around the world prize stone sculptures from Zimbabwe.

6 tanhatu (TAN-ha-too)

Six students practice reading and writing.
In Zimbabwe, most lessons are in English.
Only the youngest students use African
languages in school. Children in
Zimbabwe take education seriously.
Parents expect children to do their best.
They know that education will help
their children find success.

7 nomwe (NOM-way)

Zimbabwe's flag has **seven** stripes. The stripes are green, yellow, red, and black. Green stands for farming. Yellow stands for the minerals mined in Zimbabwe. Red is for blood. The people of Zimbabwe shed blood while fighting for their country's freedom. Black is for Zimbabwe's native people. The other parts of the flag are for history, government, and peace.

8 tsere (SER-ay)

Eight sports enjoyed in Zimbabwe are cricket, soccer, basketball, tennis, running, fishing, rugby, and golf. The sport of cricket is a little like baseball. The British brought the game to Zimbabwe. Soccer is popular in villages and schools. But Zimbabweans don't call the game soccer. They call it football!

q pfumbamwe (pfum-BAHM-way)

Nine crops that grow in Zimbabwe
are soybeans, sugarcane, cotton,
peanuts, rice, coffee, wheat, potatoes,
and corn. Farming is important in
Zimbabwe. Farmers make money by
selling their crops. The food they
grow helps feed the people of
Zimbabwe too.

10 gumi (GOO-mee)

Ten elephants play by the river. Many elephants live in Zimbabwe's Hwange (WAN-gay) National Park. The Hwange National Park is a favorite spot for people who enjoy wildlife. Tourists from around the world come to see the elephants and many other animals that live in the park.

Pronunciation Guide

1 / poshi (POE-she)

2 / piri (PEE-ree)

3 / tatu (TAH-too)

4 / ina (EE-na)

5 / shanu (SHA-noo)

6 / tanhatu (TAN-ha-too)

7 / nomwe (NOM-way)

8 / tsere (SER-ay)

9 / pfumbamwe (pfum-BAHM-way)

10 / gumi (GOO-mee)